P9-APF-409

Presented to

_____

On the occasion of

_____

From

_____

Date

_____

©MCMXCIX by Barbour Publishing, Inc.

ISBN 1-57748-647-1

All rights reserved. No part of this publication may be reproduced or transmitted in any form or by any means without written permission of the publisher.

Scripture quotations are from the Authorized King James Version of the Bible.

Published by Barbour Publishing, Inc., P. O. Box 719, Uhrichsville, Ohio 44683

Member of the
Evangelical Christian
Publishers Association

Printed in China.

KEEP IT SIMPLE

FINDING PEACE IN A HECTIC WORLD

Written and Compiled by
Ellyn Sanna

BARBOUR
PUBLISHING, INC.

Let the seeking person reach a place where life and lips join to say continually, "Be thou exalted," and a thousand minor problems will be solved at once. The Christian life ceases to be the complicated thing it has been before and becomes the very essence of simplicity.

A.W. TOZER

Take my yoke upon you, and learn of me;
for I am meek and lowly in heart:
and ye shall find rest unto your souls.
MATTHEW 11:29

4

1

ONE DAY AT A TIME

*For which cause we faint not;
. . .the inward man is renewed day by day.*
2 CORINTHIANS 4:16

Nothing is worth more than this day.
JOHANN WOLFGANG VON GOETHE

Seize the day,
and put the least possible trust in tomorrow.
HORACE

I have learned to live each day as it comes
and not to borrow trouble by dreading tomorrow.
DOROTHY DIX

As Peaceful as a Flower. . .

We complicate our lives when we borrow trouble from the future. We waste our energy worrying about what might happen tomorrow; we become frantic and pressured looking at the many responsibilities on our to-do list for the next week; we lie awake obsessing over our plans for the upcoming month.

And meanwhile we miss the precious gift of peace that God has given us right here, right now, in this tiny present moment that touches eternity. Be like the wildflowers, Jesus tells us in the Gospels, simply soaking up today's sunshine: "Take therefore no thought for the morrow: for the morrow shall take thought for the things of itself" (Matthew 6:34).

Children live the same way, delighting in the here and now, untroubled by the future. When we can find that same wholehearted simplicity, we too will know the peace of God's kingdom.

Whosoever shall not receive the kingdom of God as a little child shall in no wise enter therein.
LUKE 18:17

Write it on your heart that every day
is the best day in the year.
RALPH WALDO EMERSON

Anyone can carry his burden, however hard, until nightfall.
Anyone can do his work, however hard, for one day. Anyone
can live sweetly, patiently, lovingly, purely, till the sun goes
down. And this is all that life really means.
ROBERT LOUIS STEVENSON

No peace lies in the future which is not hidden
in this present instant. Take peace.
FRA GIOVANNI, 1513

2

SMALL PLEASURES

I thank thee, O Father, Lord of heaven and earth,
that thou hast hid these things from the wise
and prudent, and hast revealed them unto babes.
LUKE 10:21

To see a World in a Grain of Sand
And a Heaven in a Wild Flower,
Hold infinity in the palm of your hand
and Eternity in an hour.
WILLIAM BLAKE

The best things are nearest: breath in your nostrils, light in your eyes, flowers at your feel, duties at your hand, the path of Right just before you. Do not grasp at the stars, but do life's plain common work as it comes, certain that daily duties and daily bread are the sweetest things in life.
ROBERT LOUIS STEVENSON

*Children have the art of seeing things
we adults are sometimes too busy to notice. . .*

One day as I stuffed wet laundry in the dryer, preoccupied with the supper I was cooking, the book I was editing, and the phone call I'd just realized I'd forgotten to make, I saw my small son and daughter sitting on the floor beside me, completely still, their faces tilted upward. "Look," my daughter breathed.

They looked as entranced as if they'd caught a glimpse of the Beatific Vision. I looked and saw nothing, only empty, dusty air. Then I paused and *really* looked.

The late afternoon light that poured through the window had caught the flying motes of dryer dust, transforming them into a shaft of swirling gold. Each particle glinted with its own fire, a whole universe of tiny, spinning suns. "Is it angel dust?" my son whispered. I sat down on the floor with my children, and for just a moment I forgot about supper and the book I was editing and the phone call I hadn't made. I forgot everything except the wonder that can turn ordinary laundry lint into a glimpse of heaven.

by the author,
from *Motherhood: A Spiritual Journey*

Enjoy the little things,
for one day you may look back
and discover they were the big things.
AUTHOR UNKNOWN

Teach me the art of creating islands of stillness,
in which I can absorb the beauty of everyday things:
clouds, trees, a snatch of music. . . .
MARION STROUD

Be faithful in little things,
for in them our strength lies.
MOTHER TERESA

Dear Jesus,

*Help me not to be so busy that
I miss the small pleasures
You've sprinkled through my day.
Help me to notice the way the sunlight flickers
through the leaves outside my kitchen window;
help me to pay attention to the smile of
sympathy my coworker gives me;
help me to really taste the rich,
hot taste of coffee in my cup.
Remind me not to take these
tiny treasures for granted.
Give me a child's heart that sees
the lovely simple things in life.
Amen.*

I believe that in each little thing created by God there is more than what is understood, even if it is a little ant.

TERESA OF AVILA

Ordinary things have a great power to reveal the mysterious nearness of a caring, liberating God. . . . In what seems ordinary and everyday there is always more than at first meets the eye.

CHARLES CUMMINGS

Between the house and the store there are little pockets of happiness. A bird, a garden, a friend's greeting, a child's smile, a cat in the sunshine needing a stroke. Recognize them or ignore them. It's always up to you.

PAM BROWN

3

FORGET THE PAST

This one thing I do,
forgetting those things which are behind,
and reaching forth unto those things
which are before,
I press toward the mark for the prize
of the high calling of God in Christ Jesus.
PHILIPPIANS 3:13–14

A new life begins for us with every second. Let us go forward joyously to meet it. We must press on, whether we will or no, and we shall walk better with our eyes before us than with them ever cast behind.

JEROME K. JEROME

Yesterday is gone.
Tomorrow has not yet come.
We have only today.
Let us begin.
MOTHER TERESA

16

Simply Trust

We not only complicate our lives when we worry about the future; we also lose our peace of mind when we dwell too much in the past. We have all made mistakes, whether intentionally or not; we have all hurt our friends and loved ones; and we have all spoken words we wish we could unsay. The only thing to do is repent and go on.

When we obsess over the past, we are not allowing God to work in our lives *right now*. He will not only forgive the mistakes we have made, but when we totally surrender them to Him, He will even—somehow—use them for the glory of His kingdom.

In our own power, we can never "fix things." All we can do is simply trust Him.

Dear Lord, yesterday I acted before I thought. I hurt someone I care about—and now I can't stop thinking about what I did. I wish I could go back and do things differently; I wish I could somehow now find the words to erase the consequences of what I did. I keep mulling it over, thinking what I should have done differently, wondering what I can do now to make things right again. I feel as though I'm carrying a heavy weight on my shoulders. No matter what I'm doing, I'm distracted, preoccupied by my guilty feelings.

And then I seem to hear a small voice whisper, "Come unto me, all ye that labour and are heavy laden, and I will give you rest" (Matthew 11:28).

Jesus, show me if I should take some action to ease this situation—and help me in the future to count the cost before I act. But for now I'll leave this heavy load of guilt in Your hands.

I'll trade it for Your peace.

Thank You for Your rest.

4

SLOWING DOWN AND TRAVELING LIGHT

Let us lay aside every weight, . . .
let us run with patience the race
that is set before us.
HEBREWS 12:1

The definition of traveling light may vary from one individual to another. But most of us need to trim off some excess weight. We have too many social involvements, an overabundance of good but unnecessary meetings. . . . Remember the caution: *"Beware of the barrenness of a busy life."*
RUTH BELL GRAHAM

We all know what it feels like to be at rest. And we all long for that more sane lifestyle rather than being overwhelmed. But are we willing to leave the press long enough to lie down in the soothing green pastures and to be led by the still waters of His provision? That, my friend, is not resort living but restored living. And each of us needs it.
PATSY CLAIRMONT

Make Room for Peace

Our society is a busy one. As we dash from responsibility to responsibility, we seem to pride ourselves on our busyness, as though it somehow proves our worth. Even our children are busy, their schedules crammed with enriching activities. We all fly through life, fitting as many things as we can into each day.

With such complicated lives, it's no wonder we find our hearts craving quiet. We long for it so much that books on peace and simplicity climb the bestseller lists; we're all hoping some author will have the magic answer that will show us how to infuse our lives with serenity.

But we're looking at peace as though it were one more thing to fit into our lives, as though we could write it on our to-do list. But the truth is, that's not the way peace works.

The only way we will find peace in the midst of our hectic lives is if we make room for it. When we stop the mad rush, when we say no to some of our many responsibilities and take the time to come quietly into God's presence, then, in that simple, quiet moment, He will breathe His peace into our hearts.

Happiness is as a butterfly, which, when pursued, is always beyond our grasp, but which, if you will sit down quietly, may alight upon you.

NATHANIEL HAWTHORNE

Do not let trifles disturb your tranquillity of mind. . . . Life is too precious to be sacrificed for the nonessential and transient. . . . Ignore the inconsequential.

GRENVILLE KLEISER

Work is not always required of a man. There is such a thing as sacred idleness, the cultivation of which is now fearfully neglected.

GEORGE MACDONALD

5

THE RICHES OF SERENITY

The LORD is my shepherd; I shall not want.
He maketh me to lie down in green pastures:
he leadeth me beside the still waters.
<small>PSALM 23:1–2</small>

Peace is the fairest form of happiness.
WILLIAM ELLERY CHANNING

The serene have not opted out of life. They see more widely, love more dearly, rejoice in the things the frantic mind no longer sees or hears.

PAM BROWN

Our greatest experiences are our quietest moments.
FRIEDRICH NIETZSCHE

Peace Like a River

I like the word *serenity*. It always seems to me to be a shining word, like sunlight glimmering on quiet water.

I'm not the only one who connects serenity with water. The Bible also speaks of peace being like a quiet river. And David writes of the Shepherd who leads us beside the still, calm waters, quieting our hearts.

Obviously, there's a connection between serenity and water. After all, they both refresh us; they both give us life. And they both help to wash us clean of the ordinary grime and dust that darken our lives.

For in the quiet moments when we draw away from the noise and bustle of human life, we come into God's presence. Alone with Him, we open our hearts—and we are restored, brought back to life, washed clean. His Spirit speaks peace to our hearts.

And as we go back to the noise and the hurry, we can choose to carry His Spirit with us, a deep, quiet well of serenity in our hearts.

Serenity is active.
It is a gentle and firm participation with trust.
ANNE WILSON SCHAEF

Peace is not a passive but an active condition,
not a negation but an affirmation.
It is a gesture as strong as war.
MARY ROBERTS RINEHART

My greatest wealth is the deep stillness in which
I strive and grow and win what the world
cannot take from me with fire or sword.
JOHANN WOLFGANG VON GOETHE

God's Quiet Stream

I will take special notice of
the good things when they come.
I will fix my mind on what is
pure and lovely and upright.
When the heat and winds of life's storms come,
I will not fear; I know You are near.
I will not worry but keep on producing a life
that is a blessing for You and others.
Let me take time often to come drink from
Your quiet stream. I thank You for it.
ANITA CORRINE DONIHUE

The seed of joy grows best in a field of peace.
ROBERT J. WICKS

*True serenity comes when
we give ourselves to God . . .*

Anxiety and misgiving proceed solely from love of self. The love of God accomplishes all things quietly and completely; it is not anxious or uncertain. The Spirit of God rests continually in quietness. Perfect love casteth out fear. It is in forgetfulness of self that we find peace. Happy is he who yields himself completely. . .to God.

FRANÇOIS FÉNELON

*Dear Lord,
Rest in my heart. May others sense
Your serenity in me.
Amen.*

6

PATIENCE AND PRAYER

In your patience possess ye your souls.
LUKE 21:19

Be patient with everyone, but above all with thyself.
I mean, do not be disheartened by your imperfections,
but always rise up with fresh courage.
FRANCIS DE SALES

If God has taken away all means of seeking remedy,
there is nothing left but patience.
JOHN LOCKE

To confuse prayer with solitude, to say that I must have
solitude in which to pray, is a fallacy. It is good to have peri-
odic solitude. . . . But. . .prayer is a full-time affair; solitude, unless called to a lifetime of it by God,
must always be a temporary thing. . . .
CATHERINE DE HUECK DOHERTY

The Doors to Peace

How do we find the peace and simplicity we crave in our lives? I think the answer lies in patience and prayer.

We all like to be active, we want to be in control of our lives. But sometimes circumstances force us to accept that we can *do* nothing. All we can do is be patient and pray.

But notice that life has to *force* us to this point. We speak as though patience and prayer were a sort of last resort for people who are too weak or too desperate to do anything else. We turn to prayer only when we are alone and undisturbed, and we practice patience only when we have to. After all, most of us would rather have what we want *now,* and we'd rather be able to get it through our own efforts, rather than wait on God. And so we strive and strive, and our lives become more and more hectic and complicated.

In reality, though, patience and prayer should be our first resort, for they are the tap lines that enable us to find peace even in the midst of life's busyness and noise. They are the doors that lead us into God's peace. And they are the lessons that teach us simplicity.

The Tranquillity of Listening

Stand still, and lifting your hearts and hands to God, pray that the mighty wind of his Holy Spirit may clear all the cobwebs of fear, selfishness, greed, narrow-heartedness away from the soul: that his tongues of flame may descend to give courage to begin again.

All this standing still can be done in the midst of the outward noise of daily living and the duties of state in life. For it will bring order into the soul, God's order, and God's order will bring tranquillity, his own tranquillity. And it will bring silence.

It will bring the silence. . .of a mother, so deep, so inward, that in it she listens with her whole being to the voice of her children playing in a nearby yard, cognizant without effort, of the slightest change in each voice. Hers is a listening silence which takes place while she competently, efficiently and lovingly attends to her daily duties.

CATHERINE DE HUECK DOHERTY,
Poustiana

7

FINDING GOD'S PRESENCE

Your life is hid with Christ in God.
COLOSSIANS 3:3

There is so much noise in our modern world that we may not at first realize how much we need silence in order to hear. . . . True conversation, even and especially between those who love each other, requires silence. God, the great Lover, invites us into silence in order to draw forth our response to his Word.

NORVENE VEST, *No Moment Too Small*

How can you expect God to speak in that gentle and inward voice which melts the soul, when you are making so much noise. . . ? Be silent and God will speak again.

FRANÇOIS FÉNELON

The Peace of God's Presence

Looking for peace anywhere except in the presence of God is just a waste of our time and energy. God alone is the source of all true serenity. Brother Lawrence, a seventeenth-century monk, learned this secret well, as the following description indicates:

Even in the kitchen's hustle and bustle, he never forgot about God or lost his focus on heaven. He was never in a hurry, nor did he sit around doing nothing, but instead he did each thing as it needed doing, with an even, uninterrupted composure and tranquil spirit. "These busy times," he said, "are no different for me than prayer times. In my kitchen's noise and clatter, with several people all calling for different things, I possess God just as peacefully as if I were on my knees."

May we all learn to keep our focus on heaven even in the midst of our hectic lives! Then we can combine a Mary's listening heart with a Martha's busy responsibilities (see Luke 10:38–42).

Every encounter, every incident during the day is grist for the mill of the ongoing God-human communication. No activity is too small or too unimportant to mediate the holy.
NORVENE VEST

Lasting peace of mind is impossible apart from peace with God: yet enduring peace with God comes only when a man is ready to surrender his own peace of mind.
A. ROY ECKARDT

The Bible nowhere calls upon men to go out in search of peace of mind. It does call upon men to go out in search of God and the things of God.
ABBA SILVER

8

SPREADING PEACE

Blessed are the peacemakers:
for they shall be called the children of God.
MATTHEW 5:9

It is one thing to see the land of peace
from a wooded ridge. . .
and another to tread the road that leads to it.
ST. AUGUSTINE

Peacemaking is not an optional commitment.
It is a requirement of our faith.
The Challenge of Peace

God's great command is not *do* but *be!*
ANNA J. LINDGREN

Called to Spread Peace

We all long for peace. In the midst of our busy, complicated lives, we crave simplicity. But the answer lies not so much in changing our lives, as in changing our selves: When we make space for God in our hearts, then we will carry His peace with us, even through the most hectic days.

And then He calls us to share that peace with others. As we allow God's Spirit to live inside us, those around us will be able to soak up the simple, sweet tranquillity of Jesus.

As Francis of Assisi prayed, *Lord, make me an instrument of Your peace.*

39

O Lord,
Thou knowest how busy I must be today,
if I forget Thee do not Thou forget me;
for Christ's sake.
Amen.
SIR JACOB ASTLEY

Give us peace in our hearts, Lord—
and may we share it with our world.